Handling Electronically Stored Information (ESI) in the Era of the Cloud

Mini-Book Strategy Series – Book 3

Rand Morimoto, Ph.D., CISSP
Guy Yardeni, MCITP, CISSP, MVP
Chris Amaris, MCITP, CISSP, CHS III

DEDICATION

I dedicate this book to all of our clients that handle and manage the responsibility of handling Electronically Stored Information on a day to day basis! - Rand Morimoto

I dedicate this book to IT professionals everywhere who manage growing mountains of data each day and yet somehow avoid being crushed - Guy Yardeni

I dedicate this book to my wife, Sophia, and my children, Michelle, Megan, Zoe, Zachary, and Ian. - Chris Amaris

ACKNOWLEDGMENTS

I'd like to thank my driver in Chicago, Mr Ala Kaid and the City of Chicago, IL as the backdrop to the photographic scenes in this book. Somewhere along the way, our books took on this "theme" for the photos we've used in the books based on where I was when I was wrapping up the writing for the book. My "Choosing Office 365 for the Enterprise" book captured images throughout the San Francisco Bay Area. My book "Maximizing Microsoft's Azure for Dev, Test, and DevOps Scenarios" took its images from the City of Singapore as I wrapped that book up on a trip to Asia. My book "Microsoft's Hybrid Cloud: Extending the Enterprise Datacenter to Include Windows Azure in the Cloud" got its graphical images on a trip to Hawaii. So a tidbit for the graphics in this book, thank you Chicago, the last stop on a 4 country trek that this book was written... Rand

TABLE OF CONTENTS

INTRODUCTION

It's called many things in day to day business, whether it's data, information, files, content, emails, or attachments, however at the end of the day in legal terms, we're talking about content that may be deemed records and evidence, and organizations have legal requirements defining what they're to do with the stuff. We're talking Electronically Stored Information, or ESI. In the old days when things were written down, it was simple. An organization just kept track of a "shipping log," or it filed important memos in file folder that the organization periodically sent offsite to some storage facility never to be seen again. Laws and regulations did not require (and actually in most cases did not allow) the recording and use of recorded phone calls or conversations as evidence. So in the old days, when conversations were verbal, agreed to over the phone, or handled in meetings, someone would transcribe the conversations and everyone in attendance signed the transcription as an accurate account of the meeting and agreements made during the meeting. Life was much easier handing written paper documents. These paper agreements were simply filed as records of conversations.

However, in the electronic age, email messages are being deemed as records that are subpoenaed, and casual documents written in Microsoft Word and saved to a system also becomes searchable content for evidence. Even instant messages, that were once thought to be more verbal conversation-like and protected by telecommunications and eavesdropping protections have moved into the realm of managed data.

This mini-book covers the best practices as they relate TODAY to the handling of electronically stored information.

With the proliferation of cloud-based technologies like Box, Dropbox, Office 365, Google Docs, and the like, even enterprises that had great records handling processes in the past have to rethink their ESI management practices. Any enterprise that has not revised its data management, email archiving, and document retention policies and practices in the past 2-years HAS to review the practices noted in this book and rethink how it is handling ESI in the era of the cloud.

The world of cloud-computing has changed how enterprises communicate and do business, it is now time for enterprises to also rethink and update their ESI management practices!

1 ADDRESSING ELECTRONICALLY STORED INFORMATION

The practice of handling electronically stored information is only a few decades old, brought on by the introduction of computers to day to day tasks. In a very short period of time, organizations have had to address electronic information that is used as evidence in court cases. But to complicate it even more, over the past few years with the introduction of "cloud computing," the rules, policies, and practices have had to change once again. As technology has been an ever evolving field, so has the legal aspects of handling electronically stored information.

A Different Time, A Different Strategy for ESI

A couple years ago I wrote a book titled "*A New World of I.T.*" (Morimoto, 2014, ISBN# 978-1494965426) that described the changes going on in the computer industry where traditional on-premises datacenters and desktop computers had quickly given way to the new world of cloud computing and mobile devices. This change in the implementation and use of technology in enterprises has changed the use and storage of electronic information that is driving a new strategy in this new world for handling electronically stored information.

An Initial Thought on Identifying ESI

The identification, classification, and management of electronically stored information (ESI) will be addressed in more detail throughout this book, but for the most part, ESI includes electronic messages (email), instant messages (IMs), SMS text messages on phones, and documents like word processing files, spreadsheets, and the like. However, in the past few years, there have been several new methods of communications that includes "in application" chats like Facebook messages, LinkedIn InMails, Google Hangouts messages, and the like. These new methods of communications have pushed the storage and communications methods beyond traditional on-premises systems managed by an enterprise to new systems and processes. All of these new systems are requiring enterprises to rethink how they control, manage, and address enterprise communications, policies, and electronically stored information processes.

No Standard Best Practice for ESI Policies

One of the first questions that custodians of data ask is "what are the best practices for electronically stored information policies? Unfortunately, there is no simple standard set of policies that an organization can implement that is "right" for their organization. Policies vary by industry, state, and country. What is acceptable in one company is frequently not applicable for another company. Granted, if an organization is of similar size, in a similar industry, with similar goals and objectives for the management of ESI, then the policies and practices of a similar organization are a great place to start.

What you'll find in the text of this book is not a black and white guide that'll tell you exactly how to address ESI policies in your enterprise, but rather guidance around which policies apply to specific types of industries and business needs. If your business, your industry, your organization interests and needs for ESI are similar, then the policies and recommendations are a great framework to start from.

When Creating ESI Policies, Where to Start?

Over the years, we have found that while most data policy managers start with "what" and "how much", we find it is better to start with "why" and "how long." As an example, historically organizations have focused on emails and limit the storage by some upper storage limit, like 256 megabytes, or 2 gigabytes of stored content. This was because historically emails were not printed and filed like contracts and other key documents, and the storage of information was expensive, so a limit by megabytes and gigabytes per user were easy to implement.

However as more and more enterprises have moved from "wet signatures" of contracts printed, signed, and filed, along with the storage of information both on-premises and in third party cloud providers (like Box, Dropbox, OneDrive, etc.), PLUS the virtually unlimited storage capacity offered by cloud providers, organizations can no longer expect primary records to be printed or be on-premises on local tape systems.

These days, primary records of digitally signed or approved content, along with the storage of content may very well reside outside of the enterprise, and legally an organization needs to maintain control, track, and have access to the content and records it is required to manage.

So back to the original statement is the focus is not about "what" and "how much" to retain, but instead, "why" and "how long". It's having the organization begin with policies and requirements along with clear definition of how long a regulation may state content needs to be retained becomes the basis of the organization's ESI policy. That then provides clearer guidance to the enterprise what they need to retain, and how long they need to retain the information.

Throwing Out Previous Policies and Practices to Start Anew

While an organization may not throw out all previous data storage and management policies and truly start from scratch, the enterprise HAS to begin with the presumption that this is truly a new area for I.T., and that the right policies have to be put in place, not just variations of the current policies. Our suggestion has been to focus on assessing current ESI needs and requirements, and build out current classifications and draft policies, and then determine how that impacts and modifies old and existing policies and practices. By starting with a fresh view around new and current thinking, an enterprise doesn't have to try to work backwards into existing policies.

Changes in data storage, location of data, and data management have changed enough in the past 3-5 years that most enterprises find that their policies and practices require a more drastic need for change. Rarely have policies just been slightly modified, rather policies and practices are changing more dramatically.

You don't need to start with thinking you will throw out everything, but do start with an open mind that policy and practice development may need to start from scratch, and that an assessment on how new ESI management policy requirements will influence and impact changes to existing policies and practices.

The Ten Year Time Machine Rollback

When you start to think about why entirely new policies and data management practices are needed in an enterprise, simply think about the computer data environment just 10 years ago. Call it a ten-year time machine rollback, but just a decade ago iPhones (smartphones) did not exist. If you were lucky, you had a Blackberry that sent and received text email messages. You didn't have document editing capabilities on mobile devices, you didn't store documents on your pager or flip phone. Cloud computing as we know it today did not exist, so ALL of your data was stored typically on a corporate laptop, desktop, or on a network server. For the most part, everyone had a Microsoft Windows-based PC that they used, so the conversation of information being on Apple Macs, tablets, mobile phones, cloud storage systems, all of that did NOT exist.

Without all of the various smart devices, systems, and target locations where information was stored, policies and practices built in the enterprise over that decade period were very different as well. Organizations only had to focus on email messages because emails a decade ago were typically the only data medium that transferred electronic information inside and outside of the enterprise. Emails were pretty much the only things users carried around with them on their basic mobile phones of the time, which is why most existing ESI policies only focus on email messages. And it's the reason that ESI policies need to change because for many users, email is no longer their primary method of digital storage and communications today.

Focusing on the Requirements of the Digital World of Today and in the Future

Many enterprises today have users store and share documents in Google Drive, or Dropbox shares where information is stored, managed, and edited. Those shared files are not even stored inside the enterprise, but instead stored in an external storage location. If the enterprise solely manages emails and policies around emails, all users that are using these cloud-based document editing systems would not have their ESI content addressed.

Many organizations can simply state that key enterprise data should NOT be stored and managed on external (cloud-based) systems, however the enterprise has the responsibility to not only make statements of that type, but to actually implement policies and practices to monitor and validate that the policies are adhered to by users. So many enterprises these days have formal policies on use of only certain type of systems, devices, or storage mediums, however day to day practices by users include cloud-based storage systems, whether the user knows it or not, and as such the enterprise has to get their arms around these systems to truly control and address proper ESI management.

As this chapter started, the world is very different today with content extending far beyond email systems, and users handling core enterprise data using new tools, on personal devices, in ways that were not even available just a few years ago. As such, the enterprise needs to stop, evaluate its responsibilities of handling electronically stored information, and build new policies and procedures in addressing the management of ESI in the current era.

2 THE APPLICABILITY OF EXISTING POLICIES FOR THE MANAGEMENT OF ESI

A key focus of this book is to provide guidance on policies for the management of electronically stored information, however before we jump straight into creating new policies, we'll quickly review the applicability of existing policies in current day electronically stored information practices and why policies and practices of even the recent past need to be reviewed and revised to apply to the current day enterprise.

Leveraging Standard Industry Policies for ESI Management

A common practice over the past decade has been to leverage standard industry policies for the management of electronically stored information, which with a simple Web search, you can find a number of different templates for email retention policies, archiving policies, and the like. One such standards site has been the National Institute of Standards and Technology (NIST) (http://www.nist.gov) that publishes a variety of standards documents.

As discussed at the start of this book, when the storage and management of data was much simpler, having a common standard email retention and archiving policy was easy to achieve by adopting a generic template. However, as data gets stored in cloud repositories, as industries have adopted specific regulatory compliance doctrines specific to the handling and management of data in its industry, standard templates for the handling of ESI are no longer applicable. In fact, even the age of an organization's customized ESI policy documents can make all the difference. If an ESI policy is not current (within the past 2-yrs), specific to your industry, specific to the states and countries you do business in, then the standard policy is typically pretty useless.

So the ability of an organization to leverage a standard template for ESI policies is not realistic. As such, the recommendation these days is to spend the time to identify an appropriate policy specific to your enterprise, which we will cover through the balance of this book.

Current Day Effectiveness of "Deleting Everything" Policies

Many organizations have implemented a "delete everything" policy, frequently based on an arbitrary length of time, so that all emails are deleted after 2-years or the like. These types of "delete everything" policies have been proven to not be universally appropriate for enterprises in this day and age. When communications of the past were heavily paper driven, deleting emails and electronic memos was fine. However, these days, primary documents start off as digital documents, get transported and edited as digital documents, and get signed as digital documents. There may be NO papertrail to fall back on for records management, as such, deleting emails and relying on paper copies when paper copies no longer exist is not a viable solution these days.

Limiting Storage Policies for Managing ESI

Many organizations have policies where employees can only retain 256mb or 2gb of electronic mail, and then excessive information is deleted. But these policies, as with many existing policies, were developed in an era when technology systems, like email systems, were limited in how much email could be realistically stored for the enterprise. When an email system maxed out at 16gb per server, that amount of storage had to be split across 500, 1000, 5000 employees.

However today, not only can email systems handle significantly more than 16gb of email per server, users are being given 50gb, 100gb, even 1tb of storage space to store their information. For a legal defense to say that information was deleted because an email box is limited at 2gb in this day and age is no longer thinking about the applicability and viability of the data as important business records and legal contracts and agreements, but simply adhering to an archaic and inappropriate retention policy.

Storage policies have to be revised to acknowledge the expanded capacity of current day systems, and thus focus on the information, not on the outdated limitations of the information systems.

Focusing on Content and the Law

What we've addressed in this chapter is the simple reality that policies of the recent past do not apply in today's world of distributed data storage systems, and virtually unlimited storage availability. Where we'll take the rest of this book is identifying what policies and ESI practices do make sense in the current day digital environment.

What we'll start with is looking at regulatory compliance policies and laws that an enterprise has to adhere to. It is the easiest way to start the definition of appropriate content retention, archiving, and data deletion policies. With the foundation of the legal aspects of ESI identified, an organization can then fine tune requirements to choose to keep information longer, or delete non-essential information sooner. The balance of this book will focus on content, the law, and new best practices.

3 INITIATING POLICY DEFINITION FOR ESI

As identified in the previous chapter, the best place to start defining the requirements for ESI policies is to start with what the enterprise HAS to comply with as it relates to regulatory compliance and laws specific to the business and the industry of the organization. The "legal first" approach to policy definition has helped enterprises get a framework in place from which to build their ESI policies.

Starting with Laws and Regulations

We identify Laws and Regulations as our "must have policies," for the basis of ESI for organizations to follow. If a regulatory compliance states that an organization has to keep records for 7-years, then the length of time and the amount of storage required is no longer up for interpretation by the enterprise for content the enterprise identifies as applicable records to the specific regulation.

Typically, the laws and regulations have stiff penalties that include fines, de-authorization, or even key executives potentially having to serve jail time. The laws and regulations generally defined what is within scope and for how long the information must be retained, however the actual definition of exactly what content applies is up to interpretation of each organization and their auditors. So there is some variability that will differ from organization to organization.

Laws that Focus on the Transparency of Corporate Management

Some specific laws and regulations that are time based include things like the Sarbanes-Oxley Act of 2002, or SOX as it relates to the transparency of corporate management information. SOX section 404 is typically referred to by enterprises in relation to data retention and management of ESI specific to financial records and communications. Section 404 is typically interpreted to include documentation of internal controls and procedures for financial reporting.

Many enterprises have interpreted SOX to mean that all communications between executives should be retained for 7-years. For many organizations these days, the practice has been to consider email messages between executives as conversational and NOT in scope for SOX, and to further focus their scope that any and all official communications be managed through a separate records management system. "Emails" can be put out of scope for SOX, and thus completely eliminates the organization from having to manage email as a SOX applicable communications system. It is key for organizations to declare their scope, provide alternate "in scope" mechanisms for records management, and then advise applicable parties to adhere to the more restrictive scope to limit the organization's exposure of various communication systems.

It is these practices of identifying an applicable law or regulation, then addressing it in a manner that clearly defines the scope and method of communications where records and communications management occurs.

Laws that Retain Critical Data for Public Safety Purposes

Drug makers, biotech firms, medical device manufacturers and others in the FDA-regulated industry have to comply with the standards of the United States Federal Drug Administration (FDA) 21CFR Part 11 when electronic records are used instead of hardcopy paper records. The retention of data that fits within the scope of this regulation in many cases requires access 10 or more years from when the communications or documentation was originally generated.

Organizations that have to adhere to the requirements of 21CFR Part 11 are very careful how communications and records that fall within scope are handled so that the organization doesn't have to retain every single email message, electronic memo, and chat session for decades. However, for information that does fall within scope, the organization needs to have a retention policy and practice to ensure the legally stated requirements are adhered to.

Again, just like SOX, it is important for an organization to define what is in scope, and seek to minimize the amount of data that falls within scope so that the amount of ESI to be retained is inherently controlled and limited.

Protecting the Privacy of Individuals for Health Information

In the case of the Health Insurance Portability and Accountability Act of 1996 (HIPAA), the stated requirement isn't a factor of how long data should be retained, but rather that any information retained or transmitted maintains the privacy and confidentiality of the medical records and personally identifiable information of individuals. While many enterprises focus solely on length or retention (to retain, or not to retain), many organizations have to ensure that any communications that fall under the framework defined by HIPAA or other privacy regulations need to be protected.

As the data world stretches into the cloud, and access is more and more mobile, the need to address a high level of privacy and data protection has to be addressed. It's not just about data retention and archiving, but about adhering to all policies, laws, and regulations. Data encryption, device encryption, and multi-factor authentication are some of the methods of ensuring that access to certain information is isolated to only certain individuals. This will be addressed further later in this book with a discussion of specific methods of data identification and classification, as well as encryption and protection of data both in transit as well as at rest.

Privacy Protections to Prevent Consumer Credit Fraud

Along the same lines as data privacy of health information, data protection of credit card and financial information is addressed in the credit card industry's Payment Card Industry (PCI) regulation. Unlike most other laws and regulations though, PCI is not a government law, rather it is a series of data security standards dictated and regulated by a standards council of credit card industry service providers like Visa, MasterCard, and American Express. The penalty for failure to comply with PCI is more than just a mere fine, but carries the threat of having credit card reissuance costs, audits, and other pass through charges imposed on an organization, even the threat of losing credit card acceptance privileges. For retailers, online businesses, or any organization doing business with consumers, the liability for paying for credit card breaches and the threat of losing credit card acceptance privileges can put the organization out of business. As such, PCI in many cases has had a stronger motivational factor for organizations to adhere to the requirements than regulations that simply result in a fine.

The method of addressing PCI is similar to other data protection methods which is to classify and identify what information is in scope, and then encrypt and protect the information, typically through some form of data encapsulation. Organizations seek to minimize the scope of protection so that they can isolate the amount of data required for protection. This will be a common theme as we proceed down the path of managing ESI that is deemed in scope for the purpose of data protection.

Privacy Protections Minimizing the Distribution of Personal Information

There are other laws and regulations that organizations need to address as they relate to data classification and management beyond simply retaining information or encrypting information. In the case of the United States' Gramm Leach Bliley Act (GLBA) specific to the financial privacy rule, organizations that have to adhere to GLBA must provide their customers with a privacy notice that discloses how the consumer's information will be used and whom it may be shared with, and provide the consumer the ability to "opt-out" of having their information shared.

Unlike other laws and regulations, this is not a time-based mechanism where information is retained for a certain period of time. This is also not a simple data privacy process where information is encrypted and protected from external access. This is a data classification process where individuals who opt-out of data sharing need to have their information blocked from sharing within an organization.

For most enterprises that have to adhere to GLBA, the process simply involves separate databases with a default mechanism that prevents customer information from replicating between the customer databases of the organization. Customers are then provided an opt-out mechanism on an annual basis to specify they do not want their information transferred from one business unit to another. Most organizations have installed a default process that is effectively an opt-in mechanism, where customer information is not explicitly replicated between business units unless a customer specifically requests their information to be internally shared.

This opt-in method also adheres to other laws and regulations that various states have, as well as many European Union privacy laws that have opt-in (not simple opt-out) requirements. To minimize the tracking of each and every law and regulation that requires opt-in and opt-out options, organizations tend to gravitate to a more restrictive opt-in, with written approval as the standard requirement before information is shared between enterprises business units.

Laws that Protect Consumers Relative to Investments Transactions

The finance industry has its own set of laws and regulations that brokerage firms and the like have to adhere to, such as the Securities and Exchange (SEC) rules 17a-3 and 17a-4 that requires brokers and dealers to "make and keep current" certain records for up to 6-years. These rules were adopted to ensure that a tracking mechanism was available to identify who initiated a trade to establish accountability of the action and validate the accuracy of transactions.

The finance industry has responded to these SEC regulations for the most part by requiring all trade conversations to be done by phone or in person with a licensed agent. For anyone who has emailed their broker or received an email from their broker, they would almost certainly get a message that notes that trade transactions and conversations cannot be conducted over emails. This limits the finance organizations from having to keep every single email message with clients as transaction records. In terms of scope, the finance industry has effectively chosen to remove emails from the scope of these specific regulations. We will find this method of scope definition and clarity to be an effective method of addressing laws and regulations as they relate to retention and management of ESI in other industries as well.

Complying with Public Records Regulations

Many organizations, more specifically government agencies, have to adhere to various laws and regulations that require them to retain information and make the information available to the public on demand. The Public Records Act and the Freedom of Information Act are a couple laws that dictate such practices. Back in the day when government meetings and decision making sessions were in person and verbal, public records were simply addressed by making the meetings open to the public, and at most having the meetings transcribed with the minutes posted for viewing. For most organizations, the scope would include public hearings, decision making meetings, a handful of sessions in a day for the entire organization.

However, in the digital age, when email messages or other forms of communication are used in the discussion and agreement process, these seemingly casual conversations are being pulled in as public records. Just as the finance industry has limited its scope by clearly noting that emails are NOT a form of communications for transaction and trade conversations, many government agencies have addressed email communications as a non-authorized means of communications for policy, process, or decision making communications.

And not just email messages, but as file storage solutions now provide "collaboration" as a common tool within document sharing or social media tools, products like Google Drive, Yammer, Box, OneDrive, SharePoint, and the like have to have clear policies on how those tools are used to address whether all content in those tools fall under an open records regulation. Organizations are finding it more difficult to address the capture, management, and retention of conversations in cloud-based tools as users spin up various tools many times without the official Information Technology department being aware that the tools are in use. Additionally, many of the tools don't have good content management, records management, and logging mechanisms to track, trace, record, and retain necessary records management audit trails. Just because the tool lacks these tracking mechanisms doesn't alleviate an organization from having to adhere to the various laws and regulations that exist. As such, many organizations simply prohibit the use of collaboration tools unless the tools have specific mechanisms that meet the requirements of records management for the enterprise.

International Laws on Privacy, Fraud Prevention, and Consumer Protections

Much of what has been addressed so far has been focused on common laws and regulations in the United States, however similar laws, regulations, and policies exist and apply to organizations that have offices or do business in other countries. In the world of the Internet when an online retailer sells their products to someone in another country, the consumer protection laws for that buyer applies, and as such, the online seller has to adhere to those consumer laws. The consumer protections may include protections on the privacy of the individual's personal data, how products are delivered to the individual, return policies that are afforded the individual, and the like.

For organizations that may not sell products internationally, but have employees that live and work in other countries, an enterprise will commonly have to comply not specifically with consumer protection laws, but with the laws and regulations for employees working and living in other countries. The European Union has a number of employee protection laws as they relate to the privacy of employee data, the protection of their information, the transfer of their information to other countries without explicit notice, and the like.

Many of the laws and regulations protecting Europe Union citizens have expanded worldwide with strict privacy laws enacted in Japan, Singapore, Australia, touching citizens in every part of the globe. Each month, new laws are approved and go in effect, and enterprises need to keep up to date on the applicable laws in each country that they do business in and have employees in.

As much as there are dozens if not hundreds of variations of different privacy, consumer protection, and employee protection laws and regulations, most organizations can adhere to common practices by limiting scope, enable privacy protections, and clearly communicate policies and practice standards.

4 FINE TUNING POLICY DEFINITION FOR ESI

In the previous chapter, we addressed laws and regulations that we deem "must have" policies, that organizations must adhere to, otherwise the organization can be banned from doing business, a chief executive could go to jail, or significant business debilitating penalties would be imposed. In this chapter, we will touch on laws and regulations that we simply classify as policies that an organization "should" adhere to.

Policies that Adhere to Other Laws and Regulations

As much as there are dozens if not hundreds of laws and regulations around the world that carry significant penalties including jail time and fines, there are multitudes of even more laws and regulations that can impact an enterprise. These might be lesser state, county, city, or district laws enacted that organizations need to adhere to.

For these local laws and regulations, we are most aware of laws and regulations that address taxation, like city or district taxes on purchases, however many local jurisdictions have also imposed local consumer and employee data privacy laws and regulations, as well as data access rules and regulations.

For global enterprises to keep track of every single law, rule, and regulation specific to information privacy, information disclosure, data retention and the like is a daunting task. The rule of thumb for enterprises is to limit the scope, classify information, focus on personal information privacy, retain information based on rules and classifications that make sense for the enterprise. The organization should openly disclose their data management policies so that those working with ESI know how their information is stored, used, made available, or protected so that individuals can take action if desired to address their rights under the law.

Laws that Help Inform Consumers of Fraud Risks

Some of the more common and broadly referenced laws and regulations are rules like California's Senate Bill 1386 that went into effect back in 2003 and requires the notification within 30-days to California consumers and residents if their information was potentially compromised from a security breach. Most enterprises that are involved in a security breach usually have some form of notification process of informing individuals that their information may have been compromised, and many provide free consumer protection assistance as a mechanism to minimize their exposure and risk in the event that one of their customers or constituents information has been compromised.

However, this disclosure law has many holes in it that make it less black and white, along with any specific penalties that can be applied to organizations that don't completely adhere to the tenants of the law. As an example, many enterprises will state that they were unaware of the breach, so that for months while an investigation is underway to determine the extent of a breach, an individual may not be notified. Similarly, even if a system has been compromised, because of the complexity and shear volume of information commonly stored in data systems that an organization can state that while a system has bee compromised, ESI that puts an individual at risk was not compromised, and thus the disclosure to customers was not warranted. Or in the specific case of SB-1386, a disclosure is not required if the data was encrypted, which takes on many forms of interpretation whether a system was encrypted, the data was encrypted, the access to the data was encrypted, or the like that limits the need for immediate notification.

So while SB-1386 is on the books with stated penalties, with similar laws and regulations in hundreds of other jurisdictions around the world, it is more common for organizations to simply assess their business risk, and determine whether evidence shows that it is appropriate for the organization to disclose a confirmed breach and provide credit protection services when applicable, than quickly send out notifications to individuals in an unconfirmed case of data access violation.

Introduction of Laws that Address Consumer Privacy

There are many other laws that address consumer privacy and protection, like California Civil Code 1798.85 that was enacted to eliminate the practice of using an individual's social security number as an identifier for the user. For years, a social security number was used as the identifier for healthcare benefits, financial accounting records, or the like. With the enactment of CCC 1798.85, organizations had to begin issuing a different account I.D.

Other similar laws like California Civil Code 1798.80-82 is a shredding law that required organizations to destroy information that had printed content with personal information of individuals.

The list goes on and on with laws and regulations intended to protect the privacy of consumers and constituents, however most of these laws and regulations have little "bite" to them. There's not a policing agency that goes around and puts executives in jail if the laws aren't adhered to. There's not even an active agency snooping out violators and sending them notices that they are not in compliance with these various laws.

As such, this is why these laws and regulations are classified in this book as "should have" rules, because while they are valid laws, without debilitating penalties managed by active enforcement agencies, they tend to get swept under the rug.

5 MODIFYING ESI POLICIES TO ADDRESS WHAT IS IMPORTANT TO THE ENTERPRISE

In the past two chapters, we have addressed a handful of the laws and regulations that impact the need to address electronically stored information that organizations must adhere to, or typically address, so that someone in the organization doesn't go to jail and to prevent the organization from being heavily fined.

These "must have" and "should have" type of laws and regulations set the minimum bar that organizations need to adhere to in terms of electronically stored information management. With the basics identified, and the organization defining their scope to address these bare minimums, it is from here that the organization then fine tunes what it identifies as its policies and practices.

Analyzing Lawsuits over the Past 5-10 Years

The best way for an organization to determine what ESI management policies it should add on to the basics for the handling of ESI is simply look at the past 5-10 years of lawsuits that the organization has been involved in. This must include both lawsuits where the organization defended itself, as well as lawsuits that the organization initiated.

A best practice is to review what the case was about, how could the organization could have had a stronger case if it had the "right data" at its disposal, was retained data (or the lack of retained data) impactful to the resulting decision of the case, and the like. If possible, quantify the impact that having data or not having data would have had on the case and cases. While an organization may have won a case had it only had the data to prove a particular conversation did or did not occur, if the retention and management of "all data" was say $1-million over a 10-year period, and the impact was only a $100,000 settlement, it may very well have been just fine that the organization settled as opposed to incur ongoing costs for retaining information.

Data analytics has taken on a whole new area of logistics in law, similar to risk management assessments of decades past in personal injury and liability cases where "acceptable loss" is quantified and justified relative to the cost of maintaining and managing excessive information.

This is one area though that has drastically changed. Just a decade ago when the storage and management of data was very expensive in terms of the cost of servers, disk subsystems, and tape backups managing the systems, in today's day and age where organizations are able to store terabytes of information with no additional cost, the quantification of data storage and management is not as applicable.

However where data management does incur a significant cost is in the production of the data when subpoenaed. If an organization has stored information, it may have to produce the information in a court case, and to adhere to other laws and regulations relative to the privacy of individuals, someone may need to redact irrelevant data specific to a data request at the cost of thousands if not hundreds of thousands of dollars.

Data management and data analytics are significant areas of focus where information is assessed and addressed as part of the electronically stored information management process.

Patent Lawsuits Usually Suggest Data Retention

In an era where patents and intellectual property is many times more valuable than the shear manufacturing and production value of an organization, enterprises want to track, maintain, and prove the historical information on the development of intellectual capital.

In some cases, an organization wants to prove that an employee (or former employee) developed certain intellectual property while under the employment of the organization. This might include email messages of idea development, or collaboration with others within the organization on an idea or development of an idea. The extent of the intellectual property development while employed by an organization can be used as proof that an idea and development of an idea was produced during the tenure of the individual at an organization.

This proof can confirm that the development of the idea retains with the organization so that if the employee leaves the organization and further develops the idea, that the originating organization can show proof that it owns the originating aspects of the intellectual property creation. This may provide the organization rights to the patent itself, or at a minimum help the organization defend itself in a case where a patent or intellectual property dispute ensues. If two organizations develop a similar idea, if an organization can prove that the idea originated in its organization first, intellectual property rights can retain with the originating organization.

For Research and Development organizations, it is typically advisable that the organization KEEP communications, all documents, all data of its engineers and think tank individuals to prove intellectual property development started at the organization before the individual left so they can prove IP development rights. In terms of scope though, an organization can limit this storage of "everything" potentially to just the engineers or those in roles of idea development, and those that interact with those idea developers. The organization may not want or need to retain all data of other individuals, like finance officers, marketing individuals, sales representatives or the like that are not in the direct role of intellectual property development. Again, the focus is around identifying key roles, and manage the information specific to those individuals rather than to set a blanket policy across all individuals in an organization equally.

High Employee Turnover with Health/Injury Lawsuits Suggest Keeping Information

For organizations that have high employee turnover with a lot of health and injury lawsuits against them, such as shipping companies, organizations with significant warehouse facilities, construction organizations, or the like, it is typically recommended that those organizations keep ALL data for employees that are in this specific risk category for the purpose of defense. Personal injury cases typically revert to when an injury occurred, when someone was notified of the injury, and how an organization responded to assisting the individual.

While individual healthcare services can address medical care for an individual, the more expensive and time consuming legal aspect for an enterprise is the liability suit that follows. It's not that an individual seeks medical care from their healthcare provider that impacts an enterprise, as healthcare services should take care of the individual. Its when the individual sues the company for negligence because the individual warned the organization for a long period prior to the injury that there was a problem, or a situation was escalating. The organization typically needs to show that is was aware of the problem and took action. The communications, the actions, the response by the organization can minimize the organization's liabilities. Many times the communications are not done over emails, so records of conversations, documentation of actions, all of the relevant network communications need to be retained and available for review.

While retaining information may not always protect an organization from the liability of care, it is the due diligence of the organization, and the access to data to assess their risk, responsibility, and liability that helps the organization conduct the appropriate risk and cost analysis in settling a case or pursuing the case based on known information.

Employees Handling Contractual Information Suggest Retention of Information

For most organizations where a department or group of individuals work on contracts and agreements, their information is most commonly retained. This might include salespeople, realtors, purchasing agents, legal department individuals, and others that are involved in negotiations and exchange of binding conversations and documents.

Just as in other situations of data retention and management, not all information needs to be retained from each and every individual in the organization. If an organization has 5,000 employees, of which 4,500 are construction workers or factory workers, and only 500 employees are involved in back office tasks, and from that a subset of only 40 individuals are involved in data related communications, then the organization can focus its data retention potentially just on 40 individuals, not broadly across 5,000 employees.

An organization can focus its retention of information in a strategic manner, simplifying the broad storage and management of information worker ESI only on an as needed basis. Varying retention policies can be enacted so that even subsets within subsets of employees have different retention policies applied.

Other Data Management Scenarios

The assessment of past legal cases can also help an organization fine tune their data retention and management policies in cases revolving around things like harassment lawsuits. Organizations may find through an assessment of historical cases that they would be better off keeping data and having more information available to them, whereas other organizations may find that purging information on a more frequent basis may be more appropriate for their organization.

Harassment lawsuits go different ways for different enterprises. For some organizations, if they are more frequently defending themselves in harassment lawsuits, they may find that they want more data to attempt to prove that harassment did not occur, was consensual, or was actively being addressed by the organization's management.

In harassment cases between individuals where an organization is not directly a party to the case, having data that might be used in the case pulls the organization into the case by having individuals in the organization extract subpoenaed information. This could take dozens if not hundreds of employee hours to extract and provide information. And again, while the organization may not be directly involved in the case, when employee hours are spent providing information to a case, not having information as opposed to having information may be a better future position for the organization, and thus an active purge policy might be beneficial to the organization.

ESI Management is Selective by Identified Purpose, Not Arbitrary

So the end of the day, organizations should consider selectively retaining data for those employees or classification of employee where their ESI is of most importance for the organization. Beyond that, any other information retained is really cultural for the organization. Some organizations feel that information retention is up to the individual, as such, those organizations tend to have "everything" retained. Other organizations, employees have no interest keeping information that is beyond what the organization deems as pertinent information, as such, those organizations have no problems purging non-essential information.

When organizations have no specific requirement beyond those dictated by clear laws and regulations, then organization just arbitrarily pick a retention period of 1-yr to 2-yrs for duration.

6 APPLYING ESI POLICIES TO ADDRESS STORAGE CHARACTERISTICS AND FORM

Up until now, we've been bouncing around talking about the retention of data, the deletion of data, and the protection (privacy) of data, however we have not directly addressed how to define the various characteristics that we need to adhere to in terms of ESI storage management. This chapter focuses on the various characteristics and forms of electronically stored information management as they apply to policy management.

Focusing on the Retention of Information

As we delve deeper into policy management, one of the key points we'll be addressing is the retention of information. This will address laws, policies, rules, and requirements that require us to keep information, or at least from a policy prospective not allow the information to be deleted. Keeping and not deleting are actually two separate things in terms of technology implementation. When a software solution is flagged to delete information, it will go through and delete as you specify. If you choose to retain information, you would want to apply a rule that keeps information. However when two conflicting rules are applied to a dataset, which rule takes place? The first? The second? Both? Neither?

If one rule notes to delete anything over 2 years, but another rule specifies to keep any information flagged as confidential, which rule supersedes the other. While some might say it is obvious, is it really? Some organizations may have a staunch policy that says everything specifically not flagged as having a longer retention plan (such as 7-years retention) must be deleted within 2-years. In that case, a document flagged as confidential does not meet the requirement to "keep longer than 2-years," as such, the document will be deleted after 2-years.

The fortunate thing is technologies will do what you tell them to do, so if you prioritize one policy, or you specify one rule to supersede another rule, the system will apply rules as you designate.

This is why it is important for the organization to clearly define not only the rules it wishes to apply, but how each rule will interact with one another if multiple rules apply. As noted, data management software includes hierarchies that allows rules to supersede others, as well as other exception rules that prevent superseding rules and block the application of other rules. So beyond a handful of rules, the organization needs to focus on the integration of the rules among each other.

Solidifying the Privacy and Protection of Information

With many laws and regulations focusing on the protection and privacy of information of individuals, rules will be created and policies applied that will retain the privacy protection of information. These policies are also not inherently clear cut and typically require clarification on the implementation of the privacy rule.

The key for privacy rule definition is to identify not only what content should be retained for privacy (i.e.: health information, social security numbers, home address, mobile phone number, and the like) but also from whom the information should be provided and blocked. In a strict interpretation of a rule, privacy of data could mean that only the individual whom the data belongs to should have access to the information. This would mean that no one other than the individual should have access to the content of the ESI. This might appear silly why an organization would retain information that only the individual has access to, but this would apply to private documents and files that an individual stores. An individual can lock and encrypt personal files and store them in a private storage vault for personal access. Those documents should reasonably be protected and accessible only by the individual.

However many times data needs to be shared with others, such as healthcare information would seem appropriate to be shared between an individual and their healthcare provider, or legal information should be shared between an individual and their attorney. Some information that might seem like it's a good idea to share like personal identification information and healthcare information to be shared with an organization's Human Resources representative may seem appropriate as the H.R. person may be involved in insurance claim processes or the like. However in strict interpretations of privacy laws, does the H.R. person really need to know all of the details of the healthcare records, or simply just assist an employee communicating with an insurance provider or healthcare professional.

Information marked private really needs to also be marked with clarity who should have access to the information, and in what circumstances to enable an organization to properly share or block access by unauthorized individuals.

Purging Unwanted and Unneeded Information

The deletion of information also warrants additional clarity to ensure proper expectations are met in the handling of the removal of information. When information is deleted, does the individual deleting the information have the legal right to delete the information? As an example, does any individual in the legal department have the authority to delete company legal documents and records? Many organizations put in place processes of approvals before information can be deleted and purged, ensuring that key records and potentially future evidence is not improperly eliminated.

Other processes may dictate that information deleted may actually need to be retained because the information is on Litigation Hold. The information may already be designated as evidence or pending evidence in a case, and as such, the information should not be deleted. Most modern messaging systems and data storage systems provide mechanisms for an organization to put content on Litigation Hold so that even if an individual deletes information from their mailbox or system, that the information actually is retained in a journal or hidden archive, and is still available for eDiscovery search and extraction.

Furthermore, the deletion of information can go through various phases so that a simple press of the delete key doesn't permanently and immediately purge information. Commonly a delete action would invoke a warning to the individual that they are deleting information. When an individual selects YES to delete the information, many times the information sits in a deleted items queue for a period of time (frequently 30-days in a delete queue). After the content has remained in the delete queue for a specified period of time, or in the event that an individual forces the deletion of content in the delete queue, the information still resides (hidden) in the environment for a period of time, frequently 30-days in what is called a retention period. After that retention period expires, then as long as the information is not subject to Litigation Hold or other archiving policies, then the information is purged from the system.

It is important that custodians of data understand the options for deletion processes. If the custodian wants information "deleted" to be immediately purged (unless on Litigation hold), then all deletion queues and retention periods need to be set to 0. Or if the custodian of data presumes there is a retention hold period, but there isn't, then an assumption that deleted information is still available for recovery in the event of accidental deletion may not hold true.

All of the specific queues, retention periods, and other factors for data management need to be clearly understood and documented by the custodians of the data so that there is accuracy in assumptions of the expected results.

Specifying the Length of Retention of Information

As implied in the last section, a retention period may be applied to data deleted in the enterprise. The length of the retention period in some cases is variable where someone needs to set the retention period, whether that's 15-days, 30-days, or longer. Or in cases of Litigation Hold, the retention period is indefinite pending the release of the Litigation Hold timeframe.

Retention periods typically adhere to organization policies and practices, the more important factor regarding retention periods is to release the retention when the retention hold has been lifted. As an example, while a mailbox may be held during Litigation Hold, as soon as the case is over, or after a designated period has passed, a clear policy and process (that is logged and managed) should lift the retention hold.

It is important to note that if an organization has an automatic deletion policy, and Litigation Hold is lifted on content that has exceeded the age of the deletion policy, as soon as content is lifted of retention hold, the information may be immediately purged. This is something the organization needs to be aware of so that the anticipated and expected results for information deletion clearly understood.

Defining the Method of Retention

Another factor for content retention is a clear understanding how the information will be retained. In many systems, content is retained on the same system and platform that the information was originally created on, such as in the existing email system or document management system. In some cases, retention means that the information is copied or transferred to a separate system for retention.

This is important to know as information that is replicated to another system for retention typically means that information is in multiple places at the same time. When searching for information, an organization has two locations to search for data, where one location is active information, and the other location is a replica of the main information. In cases where information is replicated, when the information needs to be deleted, it needs to be deleted in two separate locations.

There is a distinct shift in how data retention is handled these days. In the past when primary data sources were limited in how much primary data a user or organization can store and save information, data that was to be retained was almost always copied to a retention system for archiving. However that meant that the organization had multiple locations where primary information is stored, and the organization had to manage these multiple ESI repositories.

With data systems now having fewer limits to the storage of primary information, the shift is to retain information within the primary storage system, thus not needing to move or replicate content. Information within the primary system can be "deleted" as far as a user is concerned, where information appears to be deleted (either by the user, or by a common data deletion policy) however the information actually remains exactly in the same place in the same data store as before, just not visible to the user. This deletion in place allows the organization to do a single search for active ESI (active and hidden content) without having to search multiple storage systems. Data does not need to be moved, nor does information need to be linked or unlinked between data sources. This new method of information management helps organizations retain simplicity of data management in cases of Litigation Hold, content archiving, applying data retention policies, and the like.

Confirming the Authenticity of Information

Lastly, a key aspect in data management is ensuring that the information stored, searched, and managed as evidence is in fact original content information. Data is considered fragile in that a user can simply open an email message, edit the message, and then save the message to the system. Someone who is unfamiliar with message systems may search for content and take the modified and edited information as fact. This could be very dangerous for a user or organization in the handling of evidence as the information may appear to be authentic, when in fact it is not.

An entire chapter addresses the authenticity of information later in this book, and how to handle and address the non-repudiation of data both stored as well as in transfer and transit. When data is used as evidence, the data should come with a statement of authenticity certifying the storage, management, retention, transfer, and access of the information along with documentation on the validated handling processes. This will provide individuals clarity that the ESI found in a search retains integrity and accuracy of the information to lend credibility that the ESI is authentic.

7 DEFINING WHAT INFORMATION TO RETAIN AND MANAGE

So far in this book we have identified that electronically stored information policies are those that best revolve around retention and management of content required by law specific to the enterprise. However as we start to fine tune policies, the next series of questions focus on exactly what the enterprise wants and needs to manage. Does the organization just focus on electronic messages? Does the organization focus on emails and documents like Word files and Excel spreadsheets? Is the focus solely on content stored on-premises in the organization's datacenter, or does content residing in cloud-based service providers also need to be a focus for the enterprise.

Agreeing on the Definition of a Record

The minimum legal clarification of what an organization needs to address for electronically stored information is information defined as a record. The definition of a record as defined by the United States government is "The statutory definition of records (44 U.S.C. 3301) includes all machine readable materials made or received by an agency of the United States Government under Federal law or in connection with the transaction of public business". Obviously United States government agencies use this definition for definition of their records, and most U.S. State and local jurisdiction also use this definition for official records.

However ESI does not need to be an official record defined by the U.S. government to be considered evidence in a case. In civil cases involving harassment or simply cases trying to develop a position on prejudice or premeditated actions, simple conversation emails, text messages, or social media postings can be used for or against someone in a case.

This is why we started the book by noting that every organization in every industry is different. What might be defined as conversational emails in one business in one case, may clearly be evidence in another case. The legal definition of a record is used as a base reference for government cases, but significantly more electronically stored information beyond the official definition of a government record is important for enterprises to address.

It is important to start at the beginning of this book to work through the clarification of "must have" and "nice to have" definition of ESI requirements, focus on content specific to the business and industry, and fine tune the requirement based on the culture and desire of the organization.

Ongoing Definition and Reclassification of Records

And while definitions for records and evidence have been written, modified, and updated through the years, the definition continually evolves over time.

As an example, telephony was originally identified as phone systems typically connected by wires. However with the proliferation of Voice over IP (VoIP) computer and internet based telephony, the definition of "phone calls" had to change. The United States Federal Communications Commission (FCC) ruled in August 2005 that broadband-service providers and interconnected VoIP providers fall within the Communications Assistance for Law Enforcement Act of 1994 (CALEA)'s scope.

In the case American Council on Education v FCC (https://apps.fcc.gov/edocs_public/attachmatch/DOC-266204A1.pdf), the FCC concluded that broadband and VoIP are hybrid services that contain both "telecommunications" and "information" components. The Commission clarified that CALEA applied to providers of those hybrid services only to the extent they qualify as "telecommunications carriers" under three points. First, providers of both technologies must perform switching and transport functions. See id. ¶ 26; id. ¶ 41. Second, providers of both technologies serve as replacements for a substantial functionality of local telephone exchange service: Broadband replaces the transmission function previously used to reach dial up Internet service providers ("ISPs"), and VoIP replaces traditional telephone service's voice capabilities. See id. ¶¶ 27-31; id. ¶ 42. Third, the public interest requires application of CALEA to the "telecommunications" component of both technologies.

These changes provided clarity that data system based phones calls were still phone calls pursuit to the Telecommunications Act and protected under Wiretapping regulations. Organizations could not require VoIP calls to be used as evidence, just as regular phone calls are not permissible as evidence, unless both parties agree to the recording of the conversation.

Handling the Access and Control of Data in the "Cloud"

As organizations move their email systems and document management systems to the cloud to services like Microsoft's Office 365, or Google's Mail and Drive for Business, organizations need to address how they will enforce their policies and ESI practices in the cloud.

Many cloud providers provide data retention, archiving, eDiscovery, and management solutions within their offerings. Organizations need to confirm that the license or subscription purchased includes the options for enterprise data management as there are differences in license versions.

And while a cloud service may provide data management and records management capabilities, an organization needs to determine whether the built-in service meets the needs of the organization. Even if a cloud service provider offers similar services, the organization needs to validate that it meets its requirements.

Impact of the Cloud and Enterprises Legal Liability

While organizations may develop specific electronically stored information policies, two factors of cloud-based services that may impact an enterprise. One, as identified in the previous section, is whether the functionality offered by the cloud provider meets the needs of the enterprise. But secondly, in order for an enterprise to manage cloud-based services, the organization needs to be aware that the cloud service is in use. Many organizations have users sign-up and use various cloud services without the I.T. department, compliance officers, or security managers aware that an external service is in use.

It has become easy for employees in an organization to simply sign-up for a service, expense the service monthly, without anyone being openly aware of the use of the services. Or for many departments and agencies, users may share content running off a personal service, so that the enterprise is using an external service without even owning control of the service itself.

Even if the enterprise is unaware of a service in use, the enterprise is still liable for information stored and shared from the service if in the course of business the service is used by employees of the organization. So the organization owns the liability of the service, without having control over the service.

8 CHANGING INFORMATION SECURITY POLICIES AND PROCEDURES TO ADDRESS CURRENT DAY ESI POLICY REQUIREMENTS

While a big focus of this book is on the retention and management of electronically stored information for the purpose of addressing compliance and future eDiscovery of content, ESI is only valid if the integrity of the information remains intact. Information security is key to ensuring the protection of data in terms of maintaining the privacy of records when they are stored so that a compromise of a system does not expose personal data that the custodian of the data is supposed to protect. This chapter will address ways that security breaches can impact an organization, and common methods to protect an enterprise and its data.

The Need for Change in Security Policies and Practices

The first thing organizations need to do when reviewing, implementing, or updating their ESI policies is to also review, implement, and update their security policies. Just as technology has changed over the years forcing organizations to rethink what, where, and how to protect ESI, so have security practices in the new world of I.T.

Most security policies were written and implemented when data was centralized and all "in-house." Organizations are great at creating firewalls implementing intrusion detection systems, and securing information within a traditional (historical) corporate datacenter. However as data is stored in cloud-based file and collaboration systems, and as data is attached to emails or replicated to mobile devices and carried around with individuals on their personally owned devices, the security policies, processes, and practices need to follow the data.

Most security policies were designed and implemented when devices were all internal, when organizations had corporate desktop systems accessing internal corporate server systems. Mobile devices like smartphones and tablets, and even the common use by executives in an enterprise using laptops or employees working from home or remote offices distributes the data beyond just controlled enterprise sites, but to hundreds if not thousands of devices worldwide.

Even archaic policies implemented years ago to address data presumed that devices were predominately Windows-based company owned systems, whereas in today's environment, employees are frequently using their own personal Apple Mac laptops, iPads, and almost in all cases their personal mobile phones to access electronically stored information that the enterprise is tasked to manage, protect, and maintain integrity and policy-based controls.

The Applicability of Device Encryption in a Mobile World

One of the changes that enterprises have to undergo is the shift away from "device encryption." Most enterprises encrypt laptops or desktops so that when information is stored on the system, someone who steals the system cannot easily access the encrypted data. The challenge with device encryption is that every time a new device is introduced to the enterprise, that device also needs to be encrypted. For users that have a laptop, couple tablets, and a mobile phone (that they replace every year or two), the organization is constantly chasing devices to encrypt. Most organizations that do device encryption solely focus on corporate issued laptops, which is great, but likely only accounts for 30-50% of the devices that corporate data resides on. What is the organization doing with the other 50+% of the systems holding protected enterprise data? Security for a fraction of systems is not very good security at all.

Email Encryption Protects the Email Transport but Not the Message Content

Organizations frequently encrypt the transport of information such as setting up Virtual Private Networks, or VPNs, so that when users logon and access data, that the transport into the network is protected. This is good in that it creates a protected tunnel into the network, however once the employee is tunneled into the network, the employee usually can simply download content from the enterprise network to their remote device. If the remote device is one of the encrypted systems, then that's great, remote access through an encrypted tunnel with the storage of information on an encrypted endpoint device!

However, again, most enterprises don't encrypt ALL devices, so in the case of VPN access, if a user can VPN from any endpoint device including a non-encrypted endpoint device, then any information that the user transports to their endpoint is simply protected data that is transported over a secured tunnel connection, but stored on a completely insecure endpoint device. Again, not a very secure end solution!

Logon / Password Only Confirms that Someone Knows Two Bits of Information

Most organizations are fully aware that simple logon and passwords are not good security mechanisms for employee identification. A logon and password combination is simply two bits of information that someone knows, and anyone looking over someone's shoulder can capture the two bits of information and then logon from anywhere.

And while enterprises have implemented "complex passwords" that requires a combination of uppercase, lowercase, numbers, and potentially special characters in the password, someone with a mobile phone video camera capturing keystrokes can easily record a complex password and figure out the logon and password combination.

The policy of frequently changing passwords every 30 days is also by itself not a complete solution as again, any mobile phone video camera can capture a logon/password combination and a compromise can happen for days until the user's password needs to be changed.

And a logon/password combination is useless when a good number of individuals use the SAME logon/password combination when they logon to their LinkedIn account, their Facebook account, or they use their corporate email address (and the same password) when they buy something off Amazon or worse yet when they buy off an unknown Website and are asked to create a new logon/password to buy something from someone they do not know. Logons and password combinations are easily compromised, and create a distinct security hole for enterprises to have to deal with.

Firewalls Provide a False Sense of Security

Typical network security systems are like M&M candies, they're hard and crunchy on the outside, soft and gooey on the inside. Firewalls and layered security provide enterprises a false sense of security, however a hacker doesn't need to break down the hardened walls and attack their way into the network, they simply need to get the logon and password of someone with network access. That executive typing in their logon and password to their VPN connection that provides the executive full access to financial records can easily be replicated on another system, or if the system is special, then the theft of the system along with a video capture of the individual's credentials provides wide open access to any information that individual had access to.

Simple Compromise Typically Provides Unlimited Access

Attackers do not need to spend time and effort punching through the firewall when they can simply compromise access of an authorized individual and walk straight through the back door. Because of all of the effort and expense an organization puts into the hardened wall security, their false sense of security prevents them from educating employees of the exposure the organization has if credentials are compromised, or a device is lost or stolen. Hours or days can pass before an employee discloses that they can't find their tablet or a mobile phone. Users are more interested getting a new device and back onto the network than they are being concerned that the lost device is a wide open access way through the hardened firewalls right into the core datasets of the enterprise.

The case of the compromise of Target Stores and access to millions of credit card numbers and email addresses wasn't a direct compromise of the Target firewalls and network, it was a roundabout access of gaining entryway through a Heating, Ventilation, and Air Conditioning (HVAC) contractor that does work on the temperature control systems at Target. The contractor had validated access, and the attackers used that entryway to slip in to the network and spend several weeks collecting information from Target Store's credit card terminals.

Network Administrators Now the #1 Target for Attack

In other attacks, the focus is not to try to penetrate the hardened layers of security implemented by the organization with millions of dollars of sophisticated security systems, but rather the new attack vectors are simply the network administrator. Network administrators usually have broad open access to systems. Their access is usually not monitored and tracked to the level of others since network administrators by definition have and need access to broad systems throughout the enterprise.

When an administrator's credentials are compromised, an attacker usually can remotely VPN into the network, have full control access to all servers and data systems, and even have access to log files and intrusion detection systems to cover up their tracks. Network administrators also frequently bypass two-factor and other security mechanisms because they don't want to be "bothered" with all of the normal complexities of access imposed on key personnel.

New Policies Need to Dictate New Requirements for Security Enforcement

With all of the vectors for security attacks, there is a dire need for enterprises to create new security policies and processes to address a more secure and protected environment. Once the organization has identified and documented WHAT they want to protect and for HOW LONG they want to protect the information, then a combination of ESI protection and security protections can be put in place.

Multi-factor Authentication to Prove Identity

One of the first things an organization can do to improve the security systems in their enterprise is to ensure they can validate the identity of users accessing their systems. If all it takes is a simple logon and password to gain access to electronically stored information, then anyone with that logon and password potentially has access to protected information. Beyond just logon and password, there are technologies that allow organizations to further validate that an individual is who they really state they are.

To truly validate whether an individual is who you expect them to be, some form of biometric authentication is typically required. Biometric uses fingerprints, eye scans, facial recognition, and in many cases multiple levels of these types of technologies. However biometrics is something that many individuals object to as an intrusion into their privacy, or has the potential for the storage of personal biometric information to be used for unauthorized purposes. As such, many organizations fall back to more traditional multi-factor authentication technologies like smartcards or other device mechanisms.

Device-based multi-factor authentication doesn't ensure that the individual requesting access is actually the individual, it simply confirms that the individual who has the logon and password information also physically has some type of device with them (like a smartcard or mobile phone). It's better than simple logons and passwords, but in no way verifies actual user identity, but something is always better than nothing.

Over the past decade or so, smartcards or device tokens have been the defacto standard for multi-factor authentication where a user has to plug in a card, or type in numbers displayed on the screen of a device to confirm that the individual with the logon and password also has a specific physical device associated with the logon information. More recently, with users carrying smartphones and with text messaging being a common method of alternate communications, the use of a text message to an associated user logon account has helped to expand the use of multi-factor authentication in enterprises.

With mobile phone based validation systems, organizations don't have to issue and manage additional devices, and users that are diligent in managing the protection of their phone can help an organization add another layer to logon and password security. These phone-based multi-factor mechanisms have become more popular in implementation for enterprises.

Movement Toward File Encryption

Once we have a good sense that the person who is logging into the system is actually the person we think they are, then the next step is to do a good job managing the Electronically Stored Information. As we've noted throughout this chapter so far, common standards used by enterprises to implement VPN access, encrypt laptops, and setup sophisticated firewall systems does very little to actually help the organization deal with the challenge of managing electronically stored information as it relates to compliance regulations and enterprise ESI policies.

Because we know that information stored on an encrypted laptop can simply be attached to an email and emailed away from the organization, or uploaded or transferred to a non-encrypted cloud service or USB device, the focus really needs to be on the data itself, not on the device or transport mechanism.

The movement these days is to encrypt the data itself, and apply enterprise policies to the data. By encrypting the data, regardless of what device or where the information is stored, the ESI itself remains encrypted. With a policy applied to the file, the policy can be set for enforcement even when the file leaves the enterprise. By protecting the data, a compromise of the email system or device, or the leakage of data outside a protected system still has the data encrypted and protected. File encryption and data policy technologies will be addressed in Chapter 13 of this book.

Impact of Policies on Laws and Regulations

While we address ESI and policies, it's important to note that policies themselves cannot supersede laws and regulations. Organizations have tried (and failed) to state cases that requested ESI cannot be provided because an automatic deletion policy eliminated the information. While automatic content deletion is fine, when a compliance regulation states that key information must be retained for a period of time, or in the case of litigation hold that an organization has been informed that a case involving specific individuals and certain information is under review, the organization must proceed with due care in protecting ESI.

Deleting ESI by policy is still destruction of evidence if required to retain information. As we continue in this book on methods of retaining and managing ESI, along with policies that drive ESI retention and removal, it is important for the organization to also make sure that the tools and processes in place also have the ability of protecting subsets of ESI as it relates to litigation hold, regulatory compliance, and data integrity protection.

CHANGING INFORMATION SECURITY POLICIES AND PROCEDURES TO ADDRESS CURRENT DAY ESI POLICY REQUIREMENTS

9 CHANGING THE CULTURE OF ORGANIZATIONS IN THE PURSUIT OF ESI MANAGEMENT

As much as this book helps clarify the need for electronically stored information management, and we go through policies, tools, and technologies that assist in the management of ESI, one of the biggest challenges organizations face in pursuit of ESI management is changing the culture of the organization to adhere to ESI policies. Users have gotten so used to keeping everything, having access to information everywhere, living in an environment where what they need is at their fingertips any time, any place, without inconvenience that users themselves are an organization's ESI management biggest challenge.

Cyber Attacks Resulting in Key Management Termination and Significant Fines

Recent cyber attacks again Target Stores, Home Depot, Sony, and others have been front page headline news as highly visible theft of credit card information, personal information, disclosure of sensitive email messages, and distribution of personal photos have resulted from the attacks. The cyber attacks not only caused significant risk in the release of what should be protected information, but resulted in the termination or reassignment of key executives in each of the organizations.

Cyber security is not just the responsibility and focus of the I.T. department, but impacts an organization to the point where accountability is demanded by the public, shareholders, and stakeholders requiring attention to the protection of ESI throughout the enterprise.

Privacy and Protection of Customer Information is Critical

The reason cyber attacks have resulted in personnel changes in organizations is because the privacy and protection of customer and employee information is critical. A breach impacts the reputation, client safety, employee safety, and overall perception whether the organization is truly looking after the individuals and/or the information that is entrusted to the organization. A lapse in cybersecurity may indicate an overall lapse in attention to detail and business responsibility. Cyber attacks have most certainly captured the attention of those in the executive office in small and large enterprises, and the policies and processes organizations take in protection of information becomes more and more important.

The Power of Social Media in the Protection of an Enterprise

Bad news spreads quickly, and as organizations have found over the past few years, social media has created a whole new challenge for organizations that didn't exist just a decade ago. It used to be that an organization could control and manage its reputation through enterprise driven advertising, marketing, and public relationship campaigns. The campaigns were tightly crafted and meticulously implemented with control throughout the process. However the work and resources an enterprise does or spends on campaigns these days can be completely undermined in a simple blog post, viral photo post, or uncontrolled social media distribution.

Reviews and the reputation of an organization can quickly change, even the structured marketing and public relations campaigns of an organization cannot undo the velocity and impact imposed by a social media whirlwind when someone is offended, disturbed, or simply wants to make a statement about an organization.

It is for these reasons that the protection of electronically stored information is so critical to an organization. The leak of sensitive emails, the early release of a memo or photo, the compromise of customer information can snowball into an extremely damaging situation. While implementing good ESI protections may cost money and not be completely liked by all individuals in the organization, having a damaging case replayed in social media can cause an organization millions or even tens of millions of dollars in damage to its bottomline, and even more so in terms of its ongoing reputation.

Individuals with the Most Secure Data Usually Have the Most Exceptions to Rules

As we look to implement and enforce policies and procedures, it is important that the goals of the electronically stored information policies are accepted and adopted from the very top of the organization on down. Those individuals at the top of an organization or those individuals with political and operational power in an organization that can easily override such policies are the ones that usually have access to the most sensitive information in the organization.

Cyber criminals have gotten smart and are no longer wasting their time attacking sophisticated firewalls and security systems, the cyber criminals are simply focusing on compromising the security of key individuals in the organization. By attacking the key executive, who didn't want to be bothered with the extra effort it takes to participate in multi-factor authentication tools, that has an override to the password change policy and thus has the same password they've had for years, that has access to all enterprise information from anywhere, the cyber criminals can quickly and easily gain access to core electronically stored information.

In this day and age when organization charts, home addresses, personal information, and other data is all accessible with a simple Web search, finding the key person in an organization is not difficult at all. Within minutes, even a novice cyber criminal can identify key individuals in an organization and begin the process of unraveling the individual's security profile to gain access to sensitive information.

The Importance of Information Classification

What helps an organization create the balance between locking everything down, that creates an inconvenience that an executive may not wish to adhere to all of the layers of best practices for security ESI management, and being able to secure key information is through classification of the information.

With the assumption that it is human nature to want to gravitate toward easier access to information from anywhere at any time, rather than trying to change the behavior of the individual, leveraging content classification and enabling more sophisticated security methods on the most sensitive information provides that right balance. Rather than treating all information the same, allow 50% or 70% of ESI with simpler access processes that individuals are most comfortable with, where data can be replicated to laptops or phones and no inconvenient layers added.

However for content deemed highly sensitive or by policy highly protected, that information can be set so that it does not leave the organization, that might require the entry of passwords or use of multi-factor authentication tools to access the information. While it is an inconvenience to access this information, when properly classified and targeted with the right purpose for the more complex access methods, individuals typically understand the need and will better accept the inconveniences.

Content classification goes beyond just the retention period of information, as well as extends beyond just an authorized user list, but should also address where information should be accessed, and the level of security required to access the information. So beyond the what and who has access to the information, the classification addresses where and how the information should be accessed and handled. This allows a policy to require a pop-up for additional credentials to access the information (like a smartcard, biometric authentication process, or mobile phone verification process) as well as a restriction on the locality of the information (which could prevent very sensitive information from being replicated and accessed outside of the corporate office).

This process is one additional step and a couple of additional areas of classifications that an organization needs to adhere to, however it does provide the organization more ways of implementing security and protection of information without having to have multiple layers of overrides and exceptions that are so often found in the security, management, and protection of information within an enterprise.

10 BEST PRACTICES AT MANAGING ESI

There are hard ways, and there are easier ways of managing electronically stored information, this chapter goes through some of the best practices that helps organization gain control and set the framework for managing their ESI.

Data Consolidation Simplifies ESI Management

With the proliferation of cloud-based storage applications like Box, Dropbox, Google Drive, OneDrive, iCloud and the like, the task of managing electronically stored information has grown linearly over the past few years. At a time when organizations were already challenged with managing information within the corporate datacenter, the addition of dozens of cloud-based repositories has made the effort of ESI management even more complicated.

Enterprises have found that if they are going to gain traction on their ability to manage ESI, that they have to consolidate the number of disparate locations where ESI is stored. We have already covered a few recommendations in this book which include data classification that helps in this effort. Rather than cutting off all cloud-based storage solutions, organizations have found if they can properly classify content, and then set policies on what is acceptable and what is not acceptable content to store in various storage repositories, that the organization can get a better grasp around ESI management as it relates to cloud storage services.

But most certainly a need to consolidate and minimize the data distribution footprint is key in an organization in its effort to manage ESI.

Managing Mobile Devices and Local Storage

Just as ESI is ending up in various external content storage systems and cloud-based storage systems, ESI is also being stored on mobile devices and local storage devices like USB drives and personal backup systems. Again, the best way for an organization to make headway on managing ESI is to manage the footprint where managed ESI is stored. By classifying content, and then setting policies that clearly state where ESI can be stored, the organization can have a better chance of managing their ESI.

The consolidation of information into a single or just a few repositories, with classification of the content that prevents the replication and storage of managed ESI on unauthorized devices is the focus of the ESI management effort for organizations.

Being Cautious of Simple Cloud Backup Solutions

When an organization has better control of the number of devices managed ESI is stored, it can also minimize the exposure to this relatively new vector of ESI management challenges which is cloud backup solutions. With the expanded use of mobile devices along with various cloud-based storage systems, solutions to backup devices and content automatically have become a major challenge for enterprises. In simple times, when an employee was terminated years ago, the organization would have the employee return their company issued laptop and any file folders that the employee retained, and the organization was able to exit the employee cleanly. However in this digital world with employees using personal devices to access and store managed ESI content, with a simple click of a button or in most cases an automatic replication of information to the cloud, and a person's laptop, tablet, or mobile phone is backed up to a 3rd party "cloud" backup system.

A good example of this is Apple's iCloud. Every Apple device comes with a default option to backup the device (Mac, iPhone, iPad) to iCloud. This is a great solution if someone loses their phone, drops their phone in a puddle of water, that they can get a new device and restore all of their photos, MP3 music files, etc. back to the new device. However from a corporate perspective, the employee who is downloading financial statements, confidential business documents, and other managed ESI content to their personal phone that is backed up automatically to the cloud, when the employee is terminated, even if the phone is "wiped" by the organization's I.T. department, a simple click of a button and the person's phone is completely restored.

Whether an organization wants to have their information backed up to personal backup stores in 3rd party cloud storage systems or not, the fact that these tools and technologies are readily available and used means that the organization is greatly challenged in cleaning up ESI data once it leaves the enterprise.

This is again a good reason why the organization needs to take into account what information should be accessed on which devices, where the information is saved and stored, and that the implementation of a data encryption technology tied to the employee's logon credentials could prevent information backed up to a person systems from being accessible after an employee (and their access credentials) are terminated.

Identifying, Isolating, and Managing Enterprise vs Personal Data

Another challenge that an organization faces is the co-mingling of personal versus enterprise data. When an employee saves business data on their personal phone that holds personal photos, music files, and personal content, there have been many challenges in court around enterprises wiping an employees personal phone in cases of trespassing or even the loss of personal photos.

Even if an employer has its employees sign agreements that the organization can wipe a personal device at any time, back to the world of social media where bad press in the court of public opinion is damaging to an enterprise in how it treats its employees.

Technologies exist that do help organization maintain a barrier between personal data and enterprise data so that an organization can wipe enterprise data without wiping an individual's personal data storage space, however these technologies are relatively new in the marketplace, and organizations need to adopt and implement these technologies as part of their ESI management strategy, and not just focus solely on setting a retention policy on an email server and feel they have done due diligence in terms of ESI management.

Controlling the Transfer of Enterprise Data to Personal Applications

For many organizations, customer contact information is a huge part of the intellectual property and competitive advantage of the organization. The names, phone numbers, email addresses, and other information of individuals is important to transition from one individual to another individual within the organization. However many mobile devices these days automatically transfer enterprise data to personal data stores, so the names, phone numbers, and other content information gets co-mingled with an employee's personal contact information.

It becomes difficult for an organization to create a split between personal and enterprise information once it is co-mingled, and the enterprise is challenged to wipe all of the contacts of an individual in fear of wiping personal contact information. Again, having a clear classification of enterprise information, how the enterprise information should be handled, a clear definition of the ownership of the enterprise information, and a protocol for managing the electronically stored information assists the organization in addressing the management of the ESI at future points in time.

Implementing Security Based on Identified Need, Not Based on Generic "Standard Policies"

As we started this book off, there is no "standard" for the security and implementation of policies, and an organization is better served by identifying specifically what is important to the organization and how the organization wants to handle that information is key. It is much easier to enforce a policy that makes sense to employees of the enterprise than a generic policy that employees do not understand the relevance to their business and roles, and thus do not adhere to the policy and practice.

Limiting Administrators and Administrative Access

As identified earlier, hackers are now focusing on attacking the administrator of the network, who typically has full access to all servers and systems throughout the enterprise, and as such has access to everything. For a cyber attacker, the focus on attacking and compromising one account (of the administrator) is way easier than trying to compromise a hardened network through brute force attacks.

Limit the number of administrators in the enterprise, and limit the access of the administrators to only what they need to have access. As much as it might take bringing 3 individuals into a room to do an administrative task, the separation of responsibilities and security makes it that much harder for a hacker to gain access to everything as well.

The organization has to balance the importance of "ease of administration" with the risks and repercussion of a cyber attack.

11 DISSECTING A LEGAL CASE INVOLVING ESI

The focus of this chapter is to walk through example cases involving electronically stored information, and the lessons learned in both the position of asking for the right information, and the position of providing the right information being requested. By reviewing historical cases and interactions, this information can be used to help organizations better prepare for ESI discovery and delivery as required in a given situation.

Who, What, When, Why – Establishing Relevancy and Cause

The key in any legal case involving electronically stored information is identifying the right information, from the right people, with the right timeline, and the expectation of what you anticipate you'll find. Without establishing relevancy and cause, ESI requests can be contested, and ESI responses will not result in what is desired.

Before selecting keywords to be searched, or when being asked to search for keywords, take a moment to think through "why" are these words relevant. What am I looking for, or what is the requestor looking for as it applies to the case. While some words might seem applicable, will they result in something specific, or will they simply result in more information to review. It's better to pick a solid set of a dozen keywords to search, than to select 100 keywords and get back way more information than desired.

We usually start with suppositions of "what" we are looking to find, and from whom, which we would like to use in the case. If we start off with a blank slate of words, they are only words. So focus on relevancy, cause, and focus so that the resulting data will support the desired outcome.

Choosing Keywords Wisely

With some initial goals in mind and with relevancy of how certain key factors can help in a case, then choosing keywords that'll support the relevancy is the next step.

Choosing keywords that are too broad will get kicked back by the judge. Choosing keywords that are too narrow may not find what you are looking for. The best words are those that in context will result in what you are looking for. Important to note is that keywords do not need to be individual words, but can actually be phrases.

Also remember that not everyone is a good typist, so if you are looking for keywords that might have common misspellings, that you have to account for common typos or abbreviations. Word spacing makes a big difference as well, whether a space is included or not included.

As an example, "pain medication" is different than "pain meds" which is different than "pain pills" which is different than "meds". But searching the records of a doctor for the keyword "meds" will likely result in thousands if not hundreds of thousands of hits.

More details on keyword search syntax is provided in the next section, but rather than searching for simply "meds", searching for "meds within 20 of depressed" can result in finding context where someone was depressed while talking about their medication.

Other examples would be searching for something like "keep confidential" than simply "confidential", or "don't tell anyone" is better than "secret". But remember, "don't tell anyone" can also be said "keep quiet" or "don't say anything" or the like, so again, going back to specifically what are you looking to find and the context that it might be couched in. You may not be able to search for exactly what you are looking for, so look for situational context that what you are looking for might be buried.

If there was a secret meeting held on Friday afternoon that only London managers were invited to, a search on "Friday near London" might extract enough emails and be unique enough to find more information of what you are looking for.

Keyword Search Syntax

Important in the process is to understand common keyword search syntax so that keyword searches can be requested to produce the desired result. Some of the common search syntax used in the industry:

- Words (exact) – These are single words like "drugs," "tahiti," or "morimoto." Effectively single words. It is usually implied that upper and lowercase apply when searching, so requesting Tahiti or tahiti is not required, but something to note in your request is that you are assuming a series of search words is not case specific. When specifying single words, it's important that the keyword is somewhat unique. A keyword of "today" or "meeting" will result in too broad of hits. Common words need to be combined with other words to have a better search result.
- Words (imperfect) - * - Using the asterisk (*) looks for words that have variations, such as "problem*" will find problem, problems, problem some, problematic, and the like. This could also address words with spaces so "san*fran*" will find "san francisco," "sanfrancisco," "san fran," "sanfran", etc. Use wildcards when there are multiple variations to the words you are looking for.
- Multiple Words – This would include use of 2 or more words, like "phone conversation," or "Friday meeting," or "read my emails". Remember, word searches are exact, so "Friday meeting" will not find "meeting on Friday," or the search of "read my emails" will not find "read my messages".
- Multiple Words (imperfect) - * - You can use the wildcard * when multiple words are used, so "Friday*meeting" will result in "Friday meeting," as well as "Friday's meeting"
- Words Within X Letters – X within 2 of Y – Another syntax is using "within" which varies from search engine to search engine, but is commonly used to search for words that are within a certain number of letters from another. So searching for "hit within 25 of face" can result in any phrase where the word hit and face are within 25 letters of one another, that can include "hit him in the face," as well as "hit his face," as well as "hit him in the arms, legs, and in the face"

Family Groups and Search Hits

In eDiscovery searches, one of the terms used is "family groups" which refers to content related to other content in a search result, commonly attachments or replied messages. As an example, if someone replies to an email message but does not include the original body text of the message, the reply might not be included in a search "hit" because the context of the reply does not have the original keywords being searched. However the reply is part of a family group, or part of the conversation and has some context of association.

Family groups are also common when content is broken up due to the use of archiving software or other tools that split messages and attachments, or some messages are stored in one location, and other messages are stored in another location. The family group will bring the message and associated components together, whereas a plain keyword search may only find a subset of messages. Family groups are inclusive of more than just the keywords found.

Requesting Just Emails, Instant Messages, and Attachments

During the discovery phase for evidence, ESI requests used to require specifically "everything" (emails, files, attachments, instant message threads, etc.) because information used to be in silos. Emails used to include only message communications. Files used to include just documents stored on fileservers. Instant messages were completely separate threads of conversations. However as technologies have merged together, it is common these days that an email message, includes an attachment of content, and the email system consolidates instant messages and stores IM threads in a Conversation History folder in the email system. So a preliminary search of an email system these days could very well find emails, attachments, AND instant message conversations in a single search.

These types of changes in the integration of different communication methods changes the inquiries and the responses to inquiries that enterprises go through in the discovery process. While casting a wide net to be inclusive of "everything," a phased approach on what ESI is requested can simplify the response so that the respondents don't hide behind a defense that "too much information is being requested" when in fact the first pass at looking at email content (that has attachments and IM conversations) may be all that is required.

Adding Documents and Files to the Search Query

Subsequent discovery requests for documents or files further extends the search query, and usually focuses on content that may otherwise NOT be in the initial query. If an organization's email is on-premises in something like Microsoft Exchange, a query of files stored in a cloud provider that the organization uses like Google Drive, or Box may likely result in content that is not in attachments or found from a search of the email system.

However, if the organization is using Google for email, and Google Drive for files, then a search of the Google for Business system will likely result in communications and links to Google emails as well as Google Drive, so a single request of Google for Business content is all that is needed.

In the discovery process, if you don't ask specifically for information, the respondents will not necessarily help you along to provide you information you didn't ask for. So being aware of the differences between files stored in traditional "fileservers" or on "computer systems" does not imply that files stored in a cloud provider like Box, Dropbox, or OneDrive will be included in the search results.

Far too often, requests use archaic terms and refer to "servers" or "computers" or "email systems" where information stored in cloud providers do not fit those older terminology categories. It is important to use current day terminology, and current day references to email, files, and ESI to ensure that the responding results take in account all ESI that exists.

Fragile Nature of Email Messages and Documents

Electronically stored information is fragile, content can easily be deleted, overwritten, or purged from a system. In the amount of time it takes for an organization to "find" ESI requested information, the integrity of the content can be compromised. As such, casting a wide net across larger domains of information to start provides notice to an organization that due diligence on ESI needs to be addressed immediately. An initial request of "all electronically stored information for employee X and employee Y" will start the process of protecting ESI.

Further requests can narrow down the scope to something that might be more manageable for the respondent to search and provide. If anything, the goal is to ensure that pertinent evidence is not altered or destroyed, and every effort is taken to ensure the integrity of the request.

Requesting Content Placed on Legal/Litigation Hold

For litigation hold requests, because ESI is stored and managed in a variety of media these days, updating the vocabulary on the request for litigation hold is important as well. As noted previously, ESI is no longer stored just on "servers" or "computers" when cloud-based systems like Google Drive, Microsoft Office 365, Dropbox, Box.com, and the like are commonplace in enterprises. ESI is also not solely stored on company owned systems like servers and cloud subscription accounts, with most organizations having employees use personal phones and tablets for business purposes, ESI can reside on personal systems as well. A request for litigation hold to an enterprise frequently only addresses enterprise managed ESI. A separate litigation hold request typically needs to go to individuals themselves with clarity what it means so that employees know that they are not to delete, modify, or otherwise dispose of ESI on their personal devices.

Additionally, traditional concepts of tape backups, hard drives, tapes, and DVDs are no longer the only forms of storage. When referring to ESI, it's important not to limit the request using these old terms. It's easier to describe ESI in more simple terms, than trying to get technical and have core information missed in ESI discovery.

Plain old English context like "any electronic communications such as email messages, instant messages, document files, spreadsheets, memos, and the like" that is "stored on any medium, whether that's on a desktop computer, laptop, tablet, phone, stored on servers, stored in cloud services, or the like". Keep the requests open so that the net is cast wide enough and broad enough to include everything possible.

Addressing How ESI Should Be Handled

Electronically stored information is not only fragile when it is stored on systems and accessed by users, it is also fragile when searched, exported, transferred, and handled in the production of ESI requests. Requests for ESI should include requests for clarification how ESI was extracted and a certification or validation on the proper handling to maintain the integrity of ESI in its "original state" that includes meta information, also in its original state. Meta information is data that is tagged to files such as when the file was saved, last modified, last opened, and who saved the file. On mobile phones and other mobile devices, beyond just time and date, many times location information such as GPS location is embedded into content. Capturing this meta information is important as it can confirm the last time a file was accessed and modified.

It is possible for someone to purposely or accidentally overwrite meta information. In the process of extracting files off of a system, an application could open the file (such as in a preview or view mode) that then writes changes to the file before the content is copied to a DVD or storage system for transport. Also, the method of transfer can show that a file was opened or saved with a new and modified date, where having the original opened and saved data is more helpful.

Proper controls in the chain of custody, along with documented processes and procedures on the handling of ESI is important in validating the authenticity and integrity of the ESI including associated meta information.

Checking for Journals, Versions, and Version Controls on ESI

Beyond just the handling of data, key is to understand whether journals or versions of ESI exist, as well as any version controls and reports on version controls of the ESI in question. Journals are copies of the original files and are important records because they provide the state of the original content. When journaling is enabled on email systems and file systems, any time content is saved, emails are sent, content is modified, a journaled "snapshot" of the content is stored. Without a journal and without version controls, if a document is retrieved, the final copy of the content may be very different than what the original file was. Someone could easily go in to a file or email, edit the content, and then "save" the content. Anyone searching on current content will only see the latest copy of the content.

Being able to reach back into earlier revisions, journals, backups of previous releases of content can see earlier states of the ESI. This is where the meta information referenced in the previous section is important.

If a document was originally created 2 years earlier, but was modified just 2 days before the copy was provided as ESI, while the current version of the ESI has some information it in, the question is whether the latest copy is a minor revision of the original content, or potentially a fully tampered version of the original. Meta information will provide a bit of history so that subsequent ESI requests can specify a direct request for earlier versions of a questionable file that includes a journaled copy of the content, a search of backup system data or other copies of previous editions of the content, anything that will show the content of the file from the time it was original created say 2-years ago and what was modified just 2-days before the ESI copy was captured and produced.

12 UNDERSTANDING THE TECHNICAL OPTIONS AND TECHNOLOGY OF ESI

When addressing ESI these days, the terms and terminology have changed so dramatically in such a short period of time that a quick refresher on the latest terminology helps to stay updated on the latest. This chapter covers some of the more common terms, phrases, options, and buzzwords as it relates to ESI management.

Electronic Mail System Terminology

Electronic mail systems have evolved quite dramatically over the past few years. When we used to think of email systems as primarily Microsoft Exchange, running on some Windows server, sitting in some datacenter, today, email has expanded to also include cloud-hosted versions of email systems. This proliferation of messaging systems means different names, different terms, different ways of referring to the age old "email system" of the past.

Some of the common names, terms, and phrases include:

- Email Server: Typically refers to a computer system, sitting typically in an organization's computer room or datacenter, running a product like Microsoft Exchange, IBM/Lotus Notes, Novell GroupWise or the like. Email servers have existed in corporate network environments since the mid-1990s with various upgrades, updates, and versions coming out every few years.

- Email Database: The email database is a file on the email server that holds users emails, calendar appointment information, attachments, etc. Just as a fileserver houses Word documents and Excel spreadsheet type files, an email server holds an email database, and within the email database are stored email messages, attachments, calendar appointments, and the like.

- Cloud-based Email Systems: Starting around 2008/2009, shared email systems started to become available where organizations could pay a monthly or annual fee, and someone else hosts the email servers and databases in their datacenter for an organization's emails, calendars, contacts, etc. The early players were small companies that hosted a few dozen organizations and a few thousand mailboxes. In the past few years, the dominant players in cloud-based email ecosystem are the big companies like Microsoft with their Office 365 offering, and Google has their Google for Business (Gmail for Business) offering. There are a few hosters that are still battling to compete against the big guys, however it's hard to compete again someone like Microsoft to host your Microsoft email system.

- Email on Client Systems: While the email, calendar appointments, and contacts are typically centralized in an organization's email server or in a hoster's cloud mail system, each user has a piece of the email system typically called the Email client software. The most common email client software is something like Microsoft Outlook that comes with Microsoft Office along with Word, Excel, and PowerPoint. Most mobile phones have some type of client software as well, which Apple provides a "Mail App" that allows access to Microsoft's email (on-premises or in the cloud), Gmail, Yahoo! Mail, etc. A browser, like Internet Explorer, Firefox, Safari, or the like can also be used as a client-based email software, with the Web browser acting as the client software.

- Email Messages: Email messages are the conversation threads of an electronic mail exchange of communications and at a minimum include the message, typically with information that includes the sender, recipient, a subject of the message, and when the message was sent. Sometimes email messages also include previous email conversation components like information from previous replies or forwarded content. Email messages sometimes also include attachments such as Word documents, spreadsheet files, PDF document files, or the like.

- Attachments on Email Messages: Attachments are files that are added to an email message, like a Word document, spreadsheet file, PDF, picture file, or the like. Attachments are not always considered part of the "message", as such, to be safe, it is always best to refer to messages AND attachments so it is clear that attachments are inclusive to requests and conversations

- Meta Information: For email messages, there's also meta information that is available for a message that provides more detail than the basics noted under Email Messages. Some meta information for an email includes information about the server where the message was originally sent from, more details on the route and target server where the message was sent to, information about the receiving system, when the email actually reached its target location, etc. This is also sometimes called the "message header" and provides a lot more information about an email than what is viewable within a normal formatted email message.

- Data on Tape Backups: Organizations with their email systems on-premises typically have tape backups or some type of "backup" of their email server, databases, and content. It's best to refer to these as simply "backups" as tape is not always the medium used these days. Backups can be done digitally these days or replicated to an offsite cloud hosted environment. So simply, referencing a "backup" of the system information captures the terminology of today's email systems.

- Journaling: Journaling is a term used to describe copies of content such as email messages and attachments where the information is duplicated and stored in an unmodified format. Journaling is common in highly regulated industries as a method of creating an untampered copy of email messages, however because journaling at a minimum doubles the amount of content stored, it is a very costly method with newer technological ways of capturing and providing non-repudiated copies of content without duplication. Organizations that have journaled copies of content will have granular original versions of ESI available for access.

- Archiving: Archiving of ESI has a couple meanings, some refer to archiving as simply "old stuff" that gets copied over to a different location so that an organization has a primary set of information, and an archived copy of old ESI. Other organizations have highly structured archiving methods that specifically moves key managed ESI to protected storage locations. Important to validate is the chain of custody and the authenticity of the archived content. If a user simply drags/drops content into an "archive", the content may not retain all of the meta information or message header information of the original message. The content could be modified and then archived, so the validity of the content should be queried and documented.

- Deletion / Retention Policy: Email systems typically have a built-in deletion and retention policy that keeps information even if it has been "deleted" off the system. When a user deletes a message, while it might disappear from the user's mailbox, it frequently is just moved to a "deleted items" folder. The message could sit in the deleted items folder indefinitely, so accessing a deleted items folder can expose content that was thought to have been deleted long ago. Extracting content out of deleted items folders can be done from backups of the email system. However some organizations set a policy to "purge" content out of a deleted items folder every 30-days, thus the deleted items folder only has the last 30-days of deleted content, and after that, the deleted item disappears from the deleted items folder. However, after content is deleted out of the deleted items folder, email systems also have retention policies that retain a copy of items deleted from the deleted items folder for a period of time, typically 15-30 days. So even if content is deleted out of the deleted items folder, it is likely just hidden for 15-30 days until the retention policy time period has been reached. Once that retention policy time period has been reached, the content is purged from the system completely. This is why time is of essence. For organizations that have email systems on-premises that diligently do backups of their systems, they will typically have copies of deleted items and even the content hidden during the retention policy period. However for organizations that have email in a cloud hosted provider, most cloud providers do not take backups of systems, so once the retention policy timeframe has been reached, the content is not available at all.

Changing Nature of Email in the Cloud

In the case of Microsoft's Office 365 in the cloud versus the age old Exchange on-premises, everything that can be done with an on-premises version of the latest Microsoft Exchange Server system typically can be done in Office 365 in the cloud. This includes functionality around email encryption, search, data extraction, legal hold, applying policies, etc. This is why many organizations have shifted their email systems from on-premises systems to Office 365 in the cloud.

However cloud providers like Google Gmail do not have on-premises equivalent versions, as such, what Google provides for email is what they provide, there's no on-premises counterpart.

Important to note is that the features, functions, and support of cloud-based systems change frequently, many times what wasn't possible to do one week all of a sudden is possible to do the next week. Updates and changes to features and functions in cloud services seem to occur every 2-4 weeks these days, as such, it is important to validate any questions or

options desired on a regular basis with someone who knows the current
state and release of the product.

Addressing Documents on Servers

For ESI that resides on traditional "servers", it is common practice to
backup systems, either to tape or some type of backup mechanism.
Organizations have gotten into a habit and routine to backup nightly and to
retain backups indefinitely. It's not uncommon to find organizations with
thousands of tapes going back 10 or 20 years. The challenging part is that
while an organization might still retain a 20-year old tape, the ability to
extract information off a tape that old becomes a challenge for the
organization.

Since backups can hold evidence, if the evidence is applicable to a case,
an organization needs to produce the evidence, which is why many
organizations have gotten into the practice of uncovering old backups and
purging them. Even if someone wants the data, the tape backup system
that was used to backup the data a decade or two ago has long been
depreciated and thrown away. Even the software used to backup the data
and the operating system that the software ran on likely won't even run
these days. So having backup tapes with no means to restore the
information is just electronically stored media that create liabilities for
organizations and have very little business value.

Addressing Documents on Desktops and Laptops

For some organizations, a process of backing up a desktop or laptop
was put in place in case an executive lost their laptop, or the system
crashed, the organization had the ability to restore information and help the
person get back up and running. However most desktop or laptop backups
are not intended to be long term backup and storage of systems as data on
these systems should primarily be stored in an enterprise repository (i.e.:
server, email system, or the like).

If backups are conducted on local systems, a process to delete the
backups every 15-30 days should be implemented if the backups are truly
intended to just be available to recover from a crash or system loss. If local
systems have primary data on them, a process should be put in place to
ensure that primary data is stored on enterprise managed centralized
systems so that endpoint systems do not retain sole copies of content.

Centralizing and managing centralized data will help the organization
implement and manage a structured ESI policy that can be enforced with
centralized policies. When primary data is distributed to hundreds or
thousands of endpoints, it becomes very difficult if not impossible for the
organization to truly enforce structured and manageable ESI policies.

Addressing Documents on Tablets and Phones

Similarly, content that is stored on tablets and phones should also be primarily centralized in an enterprise repository with appropriate ESI policies applied to the content. Copies of content can be downloaded (i.e.: loaned) to an endpoint device for temporary access, and then deleted or expired off the endpoint to maintain control of ESI.

The changing nature of endpoint devices moving away from organization owned and directly managed devices, to personally owned devices drives the policy of primary content being centrally managed and loaned to endpoints than stored as primary content on endpoints.

The Nature of Documents in Document Management Systems

Throughout this book, we've talked about classification of content as a method of identifying what content should have what policies applied. For organizations in highly regulated industries, or organizations that want to apply and manage ESI policies that are enforceable, having content classified and then stored in formal document management systems allows the organization to gain control and better manage their ESI.

Document management systems such as Microsoft's SharePoint, OpenText Docs Open, EMC Documentum, and the like are leveraged in enterprises to clearly define what content in the organization follows a clear path of ESI management, and what is just conversational content. Records are placed into the formal document management system, thus creating a clear distinction of the classification of the content.

The document management system can keep a record of conversations, agreements, key communications, and primary documents and the ESI can be managed with approval mechanisms and even electronic signatures and validation stamps to memorialize conversations and agreements.

Having a formal ESI management system and process minimizes the scope for records management, and eliminates the need to retain ESI in email messages, filesystems, cloud storage systems, and other sources of "potential" protected records.

13 TOOLS THAT ASSIST IN THE PROPER STORAGE, RETENTION, AND SEARCH OF ESI

As we wrap up this book, this last chapter focuses on the specific tools commonly used in the marketplace to assist with the storage, retention, search, and management of electronically stored information. There are hundreds of tools available, so obviously this chapter doesn't cover every tool in detail, but rather provides an assessment of the various categories of tools and common examples.

Duplicate Storage of Journaled and Managed Information

One classification of tools are products that capture ESI and stores the content externally in a third party service or data store. This would include solutions from companies like Symantec Enterprise Vault, Zantaz, Mimosa/Iron Mountain NearPoint, and the like.

Since content is duplicated and managed externally, there is a replication of all information creating additional storage of information. This means that the organization needs to purchase and maintain additional storage, which typically grows and expands over time. Organizations need to account for the cost and management of the storage.

The isolation process of ESI was commonplace a decade ago when primary storage systems like early Microsoft Exchange email systems and the like had limits on how much data could be stored in the primary system. Early versions of Microsoft Exchange were limited to 16gb of storage per server, so if a user kept more than 16gb of emails and attachments, they themselves could take up an entire email server or multiple servers in the environment. So by extracting information and putting it in a separate server, the information could be removed off the primary mail system and allow the primary mail system to be more manageable.

Another argument for these external storage solutions is that duplicate records can ensure that the integrity of the content is separated from the main application and can eliminate the risk of tampering by an errant application administrator that might have access to the primary data. The separation of data isolates the archiving, retention, and ESI management from the application.

Once content has been isolated, an auditor could query the external data store for ESI records specifying a designated period of time, of specified authors or content recipients, for keywords and phrases. Because the content is separate from the primary application, users of the primary application can continue to use their system and access information on the primary system.

In cases where archived information is removed from the primary system and stored on the secondary external system, a link between the primary and second storage system typically exists. This is where many organizations have challenges with external systems. With some information on the primary system, and some information on the external system, users are accessing content across two systems. While the vendors of the external systems provide plug-ins and agents that provide dual access, there's historically been a challenge of applications like Microsoft Outlook that every time the client software is updated, a new plug-in or update has to also be made available to the user for access to the external system.

For system integration between the primary application servers, like Microsoft Exchange and the external archive system, any time patches or updates are applied to either system, a "sync" or some form of update has to occur. Organizations have experienced countless hours rebuilding system indexes and recovering data tables to keep two separate systems tightly integrated.

Cloud Services of Journaled and Managed Information

Because of the duplicate storage on-premises of the solutions noted in the previous section, a number of "cloud services" have emerged that effectively provide this duplication of content and retention of information in an external cloud hosted environment. Services from companies like Proofpoint and Mimecast retain the storage external to the enterprise, and as such eliminate the need of the enterprise to buy and manage storage on-premises. These external cloud providers have also expanded their services to include disaster recovery capabilities so that if the organization's primary email system is offline, users can still access emails and even send and receive emails from this hosted cloud service.

The external services have simplified the storage management of ESI for enterprises, and they provide the isolation of storage so that record search and management can be conducted without impacting the primary access to the original data. These services however come at an additional cost, and enhancements along with "unlimited storage" of primary data systems now provide organizations alternatives to these external methods of ESI retention.

Enhancements Within Existing Applications for ESI Management

With recent enhancements within primary application systems as well as the offerings of "unlimited storage" by primary application vendors, the need to extract information and store it in external systems has greatly diminished. Additionally, the distribution of information between two systems, as well as the growing storage and storage management challenge has been cited by most organizations with systems of this type as reasons that the "old way" of replicating information to external systems is cumbersome and a new way is needed. Technology has evolved to provide access to archives and retained data without having to extract the information and make duplicates of information, which is the direction and movement of ESI management in recent years.

As an example, Microsoft's Office 365 cloud-based email system provides organizations a cloud-based primary email system, as well as through one of the premium service subscriptions allows users to store an unlimited amount of emails and attachments for an unlimited length of time. All of this content is stored within the primary cloud-based mail system provided by the primary vendor, as such there is no replication and no transfer of information between multiple providers. All user content remains in a single repository for indexing, search, and policy management.

Because the information is in a single source, there's no integration between multiple systems, content that is placed on hold remains in the primary storage system, and when the held content is deleted, it is simply hidden from users. This single location of information simplifies the search and management of ESI.

Focusing on Search and Management Tools

As much as technologies have improved on the search and management of ESI in the case of cloud-based messaging and document management systems, beyond just storing information, organizations need to search and extract information when requested for legal purposes.

Some storage systems have built-in eDiscovery tools to assist in the management of ESI, some storage systems require a 3rd party or external tool for ESI management. When identifying which tool is right for an organization, knowing what data sources the organization needs to search, and the requirements and capabilities needed for common search processes is important to identify.

Some organizations only retain electronic mail information. In those cases, a simple email search tool is all that is required. Other organizations have identified the need to search "all" information in the enterprise, whether that's email messages, files sitting on traditional fileservers, content stored in cloud-based document storage systems, even information stored on user's laptops and phones. The more data sources the organization wants and needs to search, the more sophisticated and more expensive of tool that is needed to do the broad range of search. This is why a couple chapters ago we suggested a process of consolidating data sources to fewer repositories, so that when a legal hold needs to be applied to systems, and a search of information is required, that the organization only has to manage a handful of sources, not dozens per user.

Some organizations want to start with doing just email discovery and eventually want the ability to search "everything." In most cases, we suggest that if the tools built into the email system does a good enough job for the basic legal hold, search, and reporting that is required, to use the built in tool and then change to a more robust tool down the line if necessary, than to go out and buy a tool that does "everything" from the start. Organizations that have done little or no content retention and search in the past will find that the search tool is the last thing the organization needs to perfect in the enterprise. After using the basic tool, those doing the searches and ESI management will realize that the challenge isn't always the tool, but how content has been stored and managed. After a few months of usage, the legal department and compliance officers will work through the enterprise to go to what we've described earlier in this book on gaining control of the information.

Initiatives in the organization will be implemented to classify information, minimize the number of storage repositories, and implement a process of retaining (and automatically deleting) unnecessary content. Organizations will realize that holding on to "everything" in dozens or hundreds of disparate data stores is just not manageable, and policies need to be put in place to better manage the storage and classification of information, so that a multi-million tool and thousands of hours by experts is not needed on the backend to search and manage the content when needed.

Once the organization has better control of the amount of information retained and the data retained is categorized and managed, then a tool to manage 2, 3, 5 data sources can be selected, purchased and implemented.

Searching and Providing Explicit Information Requested

In the chapter on "Dissecting a Legal Case Involving ESI", we provided guidance on being judicious in providing only information requested. Far too often organizations are challenged with how much information to provide, or are unfamiliar with the tool's capabilities to narrow down search criteria to focus on just what is required. As such, more information is exported and provided than necessary.

An earlier chapter identifies the technical process of using keywords and specific search criteria to narrow down information required, however it is up to the tool used to enable the eDiscovery officer to search and extract data requested. This is the important component in identifying and selecting the right tool. Take the search criteria identified in previous chapters that is desired for content look-up, and then confirm that the tool included in the primary application or a 3rd party tool being considered for purchase, will support the desired search criteria. Some tools vary in how they do search processes, with some using explicit search words, others using keyword searches.

It's a combination of having the flexibility to search in a manner desired by the organization, and the resulting information that is returned by the tool that the organization is looking to review from their search efforts. Just because a tool has the ability to search one way, doesn't mean the results are what the organization was expecting. So a simple test of the tool is important. One suggestion is to work with an expert who truly understands how the tool works as many times the resulting response was returned that did not meet the expectations of the person doing the search because the person was using the tool wrong.

Handling the Need for Privacy and Protection

Lastly, as much as information is requested in a legal case, an organization has to review how the production of data may impact other laws, rules, and regulations. Information provided may include other protected data such as personally identifiable information, personal health information, or information not relating to the case or information requested. This information not relevant to the case that falls under the protection of other regulations needs to be redacted. An example might be in a harassment case, the request is for information between two individuals to show that mutually agreed upon conversations were taking place.

However if in the course of the conversations parties not involved in the case are mentioned, with home address or medical information not directly pertinent to the case are included in the ESI, that information is protected by HIPAA or other regulations that organization needs to comply with, and that information needs to be redacted.

This is what takes time in ESI discovery efforts, beyond just finding information and providing it, it is reviewing the information and ensuring that the organization is not breaking another regulation or law to fulfill on the request in a case. Legal officers will quickly find that going back and getting rid of volumes of unnecessarily content will greatly minimize the work and effort required when a request for ESI initiates the effort to search, review, redact, and provide the information.

ABOUT THE AUTHORS

Rand Morimoto, Ph.D., MBA, CISSP, MCITP: Dr Morimoto is the President of Convergent Computing (CCO), a San Francisco Bay Area based strategy and technology consulting firm. CCO helps organizations develop and fine tune their ESI strategies, and then provide hands-on assistance planning, preparing, implementing, and supporting ESI best practices. CCO's expertise in messaging and data systems has made it an expert in ESI, and the organization is involved in ESI management systems and case analytics.

Guy Yardeni, MCITP, CISSP, MVP: Guy is an accomplished infrastructure architect, author and overall geek for hire. Guy has been working in the IT industry for over 20 years and has extensive experience designing, implementing and supporting enterprise technology solutions. Guy is an expert at connecting business requirements to technology solutions and driving to successful completion the technical details of the effort while maintaining overall goals and vision. Guy maintains a widely read technical blog at www.rdpfiles.com and is a Windows MVP.

Chris Amaris, MCITP, MCTS, CISSP: Chris is the chief technology officer and cofounder of Convergent Computing. He has more than 30 years' experience consulting for Fortune 500 companies, leading companies in the technology selection, architecture, design, and deployment of complex enterprise cloud integration projects. Chris specializes in business process reengineering and leveraging IT technologies to classify, protect, retain, manage, and analyze corporate data.

www.ingramcontent.com/pod-product-compliance
Lightning Source LLC
Chambersburg PA
CBHW061015050326
40689CB00012B/2657